Investment Strategies for Beginners

Building Wealth and Security

Table of Contents

Chapter 1. Introduction

Building a safe and prosperous future is a goal we all wish to achieve, but often the path towards it seems muddled with overwhelming financial jargon and inaccessible concepts. Fear not! In this Special Report, "Investment Strategies for Beginners: Building Wealth and Security," we aim to demystify and make investing a breeze for everyone—even those who are just starting out! This comprehensive guide is designed to imbue you with the knowledge, confidence, and practical techniques necessary to forge your individual path to financial success. Our content will be your guiding star, leading you expertly through the thorny thickets of investing, transforming the seemingly complex into manageable. Start your wealth building journey today, and watch as your finances blossom and grow. So, come on in, the water's fine! Dive into a world of hand-picked, beginner-friendly investment strategies that could set you on the secure path towards not just surviving, but thriving!

Chapter 2. Understanding the Investment Waters

Taking your initial steps into the world of investing may be a daunting ordeal. With a multitude of terms to understand, strategies to consider, and risks to evaluate, it can quickly become overwhelming. This chapter aims to peel back the layers of complexity, revealing the simplicity that often lies beneath the jargon and statistical data. So, before we separate the wheat from the chaff by examining individual investments, let's first learn to understand the environment the investments operate in, the 'Investment Waters'.

Financial markets, which include all venues where buyers and sellers trade assets, are the bodies of water within which our trading ships set sail. Understanding these markets and how they work is paramount to successful investing. While the sheer variety on offer can seem intimidating—from stocks, bonds, and mutual funds, to ETFs, options, and commodities—we will start with two major categories: Equity and Debt market.

2.1. Equity Market

The equity market, often termed the stock market, is a marketplace where investors buy and sell shares of publicly-held companies. Each share represents a piece of ownership in the company. This segment of the market is relatively high risk, but also offers the potential for high returns. Key terms related to the equity markets include market capitalization, dividends, P/E ratio, and earnings reports. You'll need to familiarize yourself with these terms in order to successfully navigate the equity waters.

2.2. Debt Market

Quite different from the equity market, the debt market is where investors buy and sell debt securities, typically in the form of bonds. When you purchase a bond, you're essentially lending money to a corporation or a government entity, which promises to repay you with interest after a certain period. Bonds are generally considered safer than stocks, but also tend to offer comparatively lower returns. Key terms for bonds include yield, maturity, credit rating, and principle.

The equity and debt markets are not the only ones; there are also derivative markets, commodities markets and currency markets. It's essential to understand these markets in relation to your investment objectives, as the choice of where to invest may be influenced by many factors such as risk tolerance, investment horizon, and financial goals.

Making educated decisions about where to invest requires understanding the economic factors that influence the overall performance of the marketplace. Central bank policy, geopolitical events, inflation, and employment rates can all significantly impact investment returns.

A deep understanding of the financial market environment also necessitates an appreciation of various investment theories and principles. Thus, we'll now delve into Modern Portfolio Theory (MPT) and Efficient Market Hypothesis (EMH).

2.3. Modern Portfolio Theory (MPT)

MPT is a theory on how risk-averse investors can construct portfolios to optimize or maximize expected return based on a given level of market risk. It emphasizes the importance of portfolio risk, asset correlation and diversification. Diversification, the practice of spreading investments around, is a key method for mitigating risk.

2.4. Efficient Market Hypothesis (EMH)

EMH asserts that at any given time, security prices fully reflect all available information, implying it's impossible to consistently achieve higher than average market returns. While some debate the validity of this theory, knowledge of the EMH remains vital to forming investment strategies.

In addition to understanding these theories, acknowledging the role of emotion in investing is crucial. Fear and greed can cloud our judgment, leading to hasty decisions. Learning to control these emotions will make for a more calculated and profitable investor.

When deciding to invest, know that there are different strategies that can be applied: Growth investing, income investing, value investing and dollar-cost averaging are a few examples. Each has pros and cons, and some may be better suited to certain market conditions than others.

Remember, this chapter is not meant to be a one-stop-shop for all your investment needs, but rather a primer to begin understanding the vast ocean of investment possibilities. Engage in further research, seek advice from trusted sources, and continually expand your knowledge. Patience, diligence, and discretion are the watchwords for successful investing. Stay dedicated to your financial goals, maintain a balanced approach, and you'll be well on your way to navigating these waters with confidence.

Chapter 3. Demystifying Common Investment Terms

Investing is indeed a labyrinth of terms and concepts, but there's no need to worry. This chapter is designed to help guide you through the rough terrain of common investment terms, serving as a glossary translating seemingly bewildering financial jargon into everyday language.

3.1. Assets

An asset is anything of value or a resource of value that can be converted into cash. Individuals, corporations, and governments own assets. For investors, assets are important because they have the ability to generate income or appreciate over time. Examples of assets include cash, real estate, stocks, and bonds.

3.2. Bonds

Bonds are essentially loans, but you're the lender. When you buy a bond, you're lending money to the organization - whether it's the government, a corporation, or a municipality - that's issuing the bond. In return, the issuer promises to pay you back the full amount, plus interest, typically in regular payments, until the bond reaches its "maturity date."

3.3. Capital

Capital is the financial resource that businesses use to fund their operations and growth. For investors, capital often refers to the financial assets or their financial value, such as funds held in deposit accounts or funds obtained from special financing sources.

3.4. Diversification

A golden rule of investing, diversification is a strategy that mixes a variety of investments within a portfolio. The rationale behind this is that a portfolio of different investments will, on average, yield higher returns and pose a lower risk than any individual investment found within the portfolio.

3.5. Equity

Equity represents ownership in any asset after all debts associated with that asset are paid off. In terms of investing, equity refers to the ownership of stocks or mutual funds. For businesses, equity is the ownership of assets after all liabilities are paid.

3.6. Liquidity

Liquidity refers to how quickly an asset can be converted into cash without affecting its market value. Checking accounts are highly liquid because they can be converted into cash quickly. Tract houses in a desirable neighborhood are moderately liquid, while a custom mansion on a large lot is less liquid.

3.7. Mutual Funds

Managed by professional money managers, a mutual fund pools money from many investors to purchase securities – stocks, bonds, and other assets. The advantage is that it gives small investors access to professionally managed, diversified portfolios that would be quite difficult to create using a small amount of capital.

3.8. Portfolio

A portfolio is a collection of investments owned by an investor, which could include a variety of assets. Portfolios can be managed by financial professionals, hedge funds, banks and other financial institutions.

3.9. Return on Investment (ROI)

ROI measures the gain or loss made on an investment relative to the amount of money invested. ROI is used to evaluate the efficiency of an investment or compare the efficiencies of several different investments.

3.10. Stock

Stocks, or shares, represent ownership in a corporation, granting the holder a claim on part of the company's assets and earnings. There are two main types of stocks: common and preferred. Owning stocks carries more risk than bonds and other assets but can yield high rewards.

3.11. Yield

In general, yield is a return on the money that an investor spends on an investment. The yield is expressed as a percentage of the total cost. For example, a yearly distribution of $50 on a $1000 investment is a yield of 5%.

Hopefully, with this lexicon in hand, investment concepts both big and small will cease to be hieroglyphics. This is the first step in your journey to financial understanding and success. Armed with your newfound knowledge, you're ready to navigate the investment landscape with increased confidence and clarity.

Chapter 4. Starting With a Strong Financial Foundation

Creating a robust financial foundation requires a meticulous understanding of your current financial state, disciplined saving patterns, balanced budgeting and cultivating the right mindset towards investing.

We will kick start this journey by examining the often underrated significance of savings, and how they form the cornerstone of your financial voyage.

4.1. Understanding Savings: The Bedrock of Finances

Savings are often viewed merely as surplus funds stashed away for rainy days. It's a widespread misconception that downplays the crucial role savings have in establishing sustainable wealth. In fact, savings are the powerhouse that fuels your financial future. Simple discipline and patience are required to make saving an integral part of your lifestyle.

To begin, determine your savings target. A recommended starting point is to accumulate an emergency fund of approximately 6 to 9 months worth of living expenses. Having a safety net in times of uncertainty provides operational room to make well-informed decisions and minimizes any potential financial strain. Moreover, this savings target acts as a specific, measurable, achievable, relevant and time-bound (SMART) goal.

NOTE: SMART goals aid in strategic planning by forming concrete targets. This practice enhances performance and

Upon creating an emergency fund, the next step is to save a portion of your income monthly. While the percentage varies depending upon financial circumstances, a good rule of thumb is to aim for 20% of your monthly income.

4.2. Budgeting: The Financial Plumbing

After determining a savings target, the next critical step is building a robust budgeting system. A budget is essentially your roadmap to financial success. It helps guide you through your income and expenses, paving the way towards a surplus that eventually feeds into your savings.

Developing a budget involves three primary elements:

1. Income: This constitutes the aggregate of all your earnings from different sources - salary, rental income, royalties, etc.

2. Fixed Expenses: Regular, unchanging expenditures like rent, mortgage payments, utilities, and subscriptions.

3. Variable Expenses: These costs fluctuate from month to month. Examples include grocery bills, leisure, entertainment, amongst others.

To create a balanced budget:

- Calculate your total monthly income after tax deduction.

- Deduct fixed and estimated variable costs from the monthly income.

- The resultant surplus is the amount available for saving.

A successful budget aligns with your financial goals and is flexible, allowing for adaptations to unexpected expenses or changes in income.

4.3. Debt Management: Loosening the Financial Shackles

In the journey of creating a financial foundation, debt management plays a pivotal role. While some debts - such as mortgages or student loans - may be necessary, others, like credit card debt, can hamper wealth accumulation.

Strike a balance between paying down debts and simultaneous saving. Begin by laying out all your debts, understanding the interest rates, and making a strategic plan to repay them. This could involve starting to pay off high-interest debts first while concurrently meeting minimum payment requirements for others.

4.4. Investing: Putting Your Money to Work

Ultimately, the decisive step towards generating substantial wealth involves learning the art of investing. It's about putting your money to work, making sure it generates returns that surpass inflation, thereby ensuring your wealth is continually escalating.

A key concept in investing is understanding compounding, a potent formula where earnings from an investment are re-invested to generate their own earnings.

NOTE: In the words of Albert Einstein, "Compound interest is the eighth wonder of the world. He who understands it, earns

Propelling forward from here involves gaining an understanding of various asset classes, risk management, and forming a diversified portfolio. Investing isn't a quick-rich scheme, it's a commitment to long-term sustainable success.

4.5. The Right Mindset: Building Long Term

Financial freedom is not an overnight accomplishment; it's a journey that requires patience and perseverance. It requires you to stay committed to your goals, even in the face of economic downturns or personal setbacks.

A great financial foundation is a tango between informed decision-making and personal discipline. Hence, continuously educating yourself is paramount.

In conclusion, setting up a strong financial foundation is akin to building a sturdy house - investors need to start with a solid base, build with good quality materials, and consistently maintain the structure to ensure it lasts a lifetime. Regardless of your financial expertise, everyone can benefit from going back to the basics, and this chapter is just the beginning of your financial edify.

Chapter 5. Diversity: The Key to a Balanced Investment Portfolio

Just as you wouldn't put all your eggs in one basket, you wouldn't place all your investment capital into a single asset class. If you do, you could be exposing your portfolio, and subsequently your financial health, to potential hazards or losses. This is where the magic of diversification comes in. Diversification is considered one of the fundamental principles of investing. It's a risk management strategy that involves spreading investments among various different assets or asset classes to minimize exposure to any single investment.

5.1. The Rationale Behind Diversification

You might wonder why you should bother diversifying your portfolio rather than just choosing a few good stocks and sticking with those. The answer is that even the best stocks can alarmingly plummet in value, and in such cases, not having all your money in one basket can soften the blow and prevent catastrophic losses. Different assets will perform differently in varying market conditions. By diversifying, you are spreading the risk and ensuring that poor performance by some assets can be offset by better performance by others.

Another key benefit of diversification is the potential to increase your overall return. If you've chosen a mix of assets, some of which are more volatile and potentially more profitable than others, you might realize an overall higher return on investment than if you stuck with more conservative, low-risk assets.

5.2. Asset Allocation: The Engine of Diversification

The first step towards diversification is determining your asset allocation, that is, the way you divide your investments among different asset classes such as stocks, bonds, and cash equivalents. The right allocation for you will depend on your financial goals, your risk tolerance, and your investment horizon.

Stocks often provide the highest potential for growth and are thus an attractive choice for those with a long-term investment horizon and a high tolerance for risk. Bonds, on the other hand, can provide a stable income stream and are particularly appealing to those nearing retirement, who require more stability. Cash equivalents like CDs and money market funds offer the lowest risk but also lower returns. They can be an excellent choice for preserving capital.

Deploying these three asset types in a balanced way contributes to an efficient diversification strategy. Notably, the percentages of each asset class within your portfolio will vary depending on your personal investment elements. Therefore, it's essential to frequently reevaluate these allocations as market conditions, personal circumstances, and financial goals may change.

5.3. The Role of Sub-Asset Classes

Diversification doesn't stop with your primary asset allocation. Within each asset class (stocks, bonds, cash equivalents), there are various subdivisions, known as sub-asset classes. In the realm of stocks, these include categories like international stocks, small-cap stocks, large-cap stocks, growth stocks, and value stocks, to name a few. Bond categories also have subdivisions—corporate, municipal, treasury, short-term, long-term, and others. Each sub-asset class carries a distinct set of risks and rewards, providing an extra layer of diversification.

5.4. Rebalancing: Keeping Your Portfolio On Track

Once you've allocated your assets and selected your primary asset and sub-asset classes, it's critical not to neglect monitoring your portfolio. Over time, shifts in market values can skew your original asset allocation, leaving you with a portfolio risk level that's different from your initial intention.

Rebalancing, or readjusting your portfolio back to its original asset allocation, is a way to pull everything back into alignment. This might involve selling certain investments that have done well and purchasing others that have underperformed—a belief in the philosophy of "buy low and sell high." Rebalancing can be done at set intervals, like annually or semi-annually, or whenever your asset allocation veers off course by a certain percentage.

5.5. The Risks Involved

It's important to note that while diversification can help manage risk and reduce the volatility of an asset mix over time, it doesn't assure a profit or guarantee against loss. It's always crucial to remember market risk is inherent in all investments.

5.6. Diversifying With Mutual and Exchange-Traded Funds (ETFs)

One excellent way to immediately diversify a portfolio is through mutual funds or exchange-traded funds (ETFs). A mutual fund is basically a bucket of various different securities (like stocks or bonds) that an investor can buy into. The same principle applies to ETFs.

These funds can offer instant diversification as they primarily deal with a multitude of various securities, helping spread the risk compared to individual stocks or bonds. For a beginner, they present an efficient and hassle-free way to access diversified investments.

Investment strategies vary greatly and are highly dependent on individual financial goals and risk tolerances. However, diversification is a key principle that remains relevant regardless of the investing context. Whether you're just planting the first seeds or nurturing a growing portfolio, it's crucial to remember the potential benefits of diversification and continually optimize your strategy for balanced growth.

Chapter 6. Bonds, Stocks, and Mutual Funds: What's the Difference?

To start unravelling the knot of investment language and terminology, it is important that we understand a trio of fundamental instruments. These are bonds, stocks, and mutual funds. There is no doubt you've heard these terms used often in financial discourse, but comprehending their full implications, opportunities, and risks is a bit more strenuous. Our goal is to present you with a nuanced, clear, and comprehensive understanding of these critical tools.

6.1. Bonds 101

A bond is similar to loaning money. When you buy a bond, you're effectively loaning whatever amount you paid to the entity that issued the bond, be it a corporation, a city, or even the United States government. In return for this loan, the issuer of the bond agrees to pay you interest over a set period of time. At the end of this period—the 'term' of the bond—the issuer repays the original loan amount. This is often referred to as the 'principal'. The interest payments offered by bonds offer a predictable stream of income, making them a popular choice among investors seeking stability.

Bonds are also ranked by credit rating agencies like Standard & Poor's and Moody's, offering an insight into the financial health and creditworthiness of the issuers. The better the rating, the less likely it is that the issuer will default, providing more security for your investment.

6.2. Stocks Uncovered

In essence, purchasing a stock means buying a tiny slice of ownership in a company. When you own a share (or shares) of a company's stock, you own a part of the company, and will share in its success... or failure. This is where the risk and reward aspect of stocks comes into play.

When a company does well, the value of its stock grows. If you've invested in the stock of that company, your investment grows too. Conversely, if the company stumbles, the value of the stock might fall. Stocks offer a higher potential for profit than bonds, but also a higher level of risk. It is this balance that investors must consider.

Companies may also choose to distribute profits back to their shareholders in the form of dividends. This provides an additional source of income for the investor.

6.3. Mutual Funds Explained

A mutual fund is an investment vehicle that pools together money from a multitude of investors to buy a diversified portfolio of investments, which can include stocks, bonds, money market investments and other assets. This allows investors to own a small piece of a large, varied collection of investments, making mutual funds one of the easiest and most cost-effective ways to diversify your portfolio.

There are different types of mutual funds each with its own risk and reward level. Most mutual funds are managed by professional fund managers who make decisions on what assets to buy or sell within the fund's portfolio according to the fund's investment strategy.

6.4. Comparing the Trio

Understanding how each of these investment tools works individually is crucial, but equally important is appreciating how they can operate together and compare to each other.

To summarize: bonds are predictable but offer low returns, stocks offer significantly higher potential returns but with added risk, and mutual funds provide diversification but also come with management fees.

Investing is not a one-size-fits-all game. Different people have different financial goals, comfort with risk, and investment horizons. Learning about the trio of bonds, stocks, and mutual funds gives you knowledge to decide how each fits into your investment strategy.

People near retirement, for instance, might lean towards the safety of bonds, sacrificing potential for profit in exchange for more security when their salary income is about to cease. Younger investors might shoulder the risk of stocks for the chance at reaping greater profits over decades. Amongst all of this, mutual funds offer a way to help spread risk while allowing a degree of professional management.

Do remember, though, that as with any investment, none of these options guarantees profits. It's important for every investor to do their research, understand their comfort with risk, and perhaps most importantly, consult with a financial adviser. This guide, we hope, serves as a baseline for that research.

With a basic understanding of the fundamental building blocks of bonds, stocks, and mutual funds, we are set to delve deeper into the world of investing. Armed with this knowledge, you're better equipped to navigate the complex landscape of investing, and to start considering what it means to build an investment portfolio that suits your needs, goals, and risk tolerance.

Investing is a journey. It's a path paved the hard way, filled with challenges and potential pitfalls, but also with enormous opportunities. Embrace the challenge, and move forward empowered and enriched. Perhaps the most essential phrase in investing is 'Know what you're investing in,' and in understanding bonds, stocks, and mutual funds, you're already making strides on that journey.

Chapter 7. Making Sense of Risk and Reward

For any budding investor, understanding the concept of risk and reward is fundamental. This relationship forms the crux of all investing decisions, making it imperative you master it before stepping into the investment world. Comprehending what risk and reward entail, how they interact, and what you can do to mange them lays the crucial groundwork for a fruitful investment portfolio.

7.1. The Concept of Risk

In the realm of investments, 'risk' refers to the probability of an investment returning less than expected, or even losing its value completely. Every investment comes with a certain level of risk, which can sometimes feel like a gamble.

Consider buying shares in a company. If the company performs well, the value of those shares will likely increase and so will your investment. However, if the company struggles or fails, the value of the shares could decrease, resulting in a loss.

There are various types of risk you should be cognizant of:

1. Market Risk: This is the risk that the market as a whole will decrease, bringing down the value of your investments along with it.

2. Company Risk: This refers to the risk that a particular company you've invested in will perform poorly or go bust.

3. Interest Rate Risk: This is the risk associated with changes in the interest rates that could negatively impact your investments.

4. Inflation Risk: This is the risk of rising prices affecting your purchasing power.

5. Liquidity Risk: It's the risk that you may not be able to sell your investment when you wish to.

Remember, different types of investments entail different levels of risk. Generally, the potential return on an investment goes up with the level of risk. Which brings us to the concept of reward.

7.2. The Concept of Reward

In investing terms, 'reward' is the potential return you get on your investment. It's the reason you invest in the first place.

There are typically two types of rewards when it comes to investments—the return on your investment or the income you generate from the investment. The return on investment (ROI) is essentially the profit you make. Income from investments can come in various forms such as dividends from shares, rent from real estate, or interest from bonds.

7.3. Risk-Reward Ratio

The risk-reward ratio is a critical concept you need to grasp as a budding investor. Simply put, it's a measure of the potential reward for every dollar risked on an investment.

A risk-reward ratio of 1:3 signifies that for every dollar risked, the expected return is three dollars. However, high-reward investments also come with high risk. The correlation between risk and reward is, therefore, direct and proportionate.

7.4. Risk Profile and Tolerance

Every investor is unique, and so are their circumstances, financial goals, and risk tolerance. Understanding your risk tolerance can guide your investment decisions effectively.

Here are a few factors that might influence your risk tolerance:

1. Age: Younger individuals may be able to bear more risk because they have more time to recover from potential losses.

2. Financial Position: Those with more disposable income or a stable income stream can generally tolerate more risk.

3. Financial Goals: Depending on whether you're saving for a short-term goal (like a vacation) or a long-term goal (like retirement), the level of risk you can tolerate will likely change.

4. Individual Personality: Some people are more comfortable with risk than others.

7.5. Managing Risk and Reward

Now that you're familiar with risk, reward, and their relationship, the question arises—how do you manage your risk while seeking rewards?

1. Diversification: Instead of putting all your eggs in one basket, spread out your investments across various sectors, asset classes, and geographical locations. This can help reduce the impact of one poor-performing investment on your overall portfolio.

2. Asset Allocation: This involves distributing your investment across various asset classes such as stocks, bonds, and cash equivalents to diversify risk.

3. Regular Monitoring: Stay on top of financial news and markets trends. Regularly review and adjust your portfolio as needed.

4. Seek Professional Advice: A professional financial advisor can help tailor an investment strategy that fits your unique risk-reward profile and helps you achieve your financial goals.

This discussion on risk and reward is your first leap into the fascinating world of investing. Risk is not to be feared but understood, managed, and even embraced. It's the catalyst that drives potential returns. In making sense of risk and reward, you've begun to arm yourself with essential tools to build your financial future confidently.

With a balanced appreciation for these principles, your well-planned investment journey may just turn out to be a rewarding adventure. Let's dive deeper into the intricacies of investing as we explore further in the subsequent sections. Remember, the goal is not to avoid risk, but to make informed, strategic decisions that increase your odds of reaping satisfying rewards.

Chapter 8. The Power of Compound Interest

In the realm of finance, Albert Einstein is often quoted as saying, "Compound interest is the eighth wonder of the world. He who understands it, earns it; he who doesn't, pays it." Such an endorsement from a man synonymous with genius merits comprehensive understanding of compound interest. So, let's delve deeper into this powerful financial element—its workings, its potential and how it can be a significant tool in your investment arsenal.

8.1. Understanding Compound Interest

Compound interest is the interest calculated on the initial principal, which also includes all the accumulated interest from previous periods. The calculation does not consider the principal alone, but the sum of the principal and the interest that has accumulated over preceding periods. This aggregation is the reason why compound interest amplifies your earnings or your debts.

Unlike simple interest, where the percentage is calculated on the principal amount alone, compound interest amplifies the growth of the accrued interest too. When compounded annually, the interest accumulated over the year is added to the principal. For the forthcoming year, the interest will be computed on this new principal.

The formula for compound interest is:

$$A = P (1 + r/n)^{(nt)}$$

Where:

- A is the amount of money earned after n years, including interest.

- P is the principal amount (the initial amount you start with).

- r is the annual interest rate (as a decimal).

- n is the number of times that interest is compounded per year.

- t is the time the money is invested for, in years.

Observe that n and t are both incorporated in the formula, highlighting the important role time and frequency of compounding play in the growth of your investment.

8.2. The Magic of Compounding

To truly appreciate the power of compound interest, you should examine its impact over time. Consider an investment of $10,000 compounded annually at a rate of 5% and see how it grows over the years.

Year 0: $10,000
 Year 1: $10,500
 Year 2: $11,025
 Year 3: $11,576
 ... and so on

The numbers might not seem striking initially. You gain only $500 in the first year, and the interest raises incrementally over the years.

But this principal stored safely in an interest-bearing account, untouched, given enough time, can lead to astonishing results due to the compound nature of the interest.

By year 30: $43,198.90
 By year 40: $70,399.82
 By year 50: $114,674.56

As we can see, our initial principal of $10,000 has multiplied manifold over the years, courtesy of compound interest. The gains are relatively modest in the early years. However, over long periods, the effects of compounding become more pronounced. This dramatic increase affirms the concept that the rewards of compounding interest are reaped largely by those who start investing early and allow the magic of compounding to act over time.

8.3. Frequency of Compounding

Moving ahead, another aspect of compound interest is the frequency of compounding. This relates to the number of times interest is added to the principal in a year. Interest can be compounded annually, semi-annually, quarterly, monthly, or even daily, and the more frequently it's done, the more beneficial it is for the investment.

Considering the same principal amount of $10,000 with an interest rate of 5%, but now compounded semi-annually for 20 years, the growth will look different.

Semiannual compounding: $27,126

This is more than the annual compound interest over the same period, which will be $26,532. Compare this to quarterly compounding, which totals $27,193–a gain of approximately $67 from semi-annual compounding and a gain of roughly $660 from annual compounding.

The impact of compound interest gets more dramatic as the frequency of compounding increases and continues over a longer period.

8.4. Compound Interest: An Investor's Best Friend

For investors, compound interest is a potent ally. The principle of compounding is straightforward: reinvest the earnings from an investment for a prolonged period, and the returns accumulate dramatically.

If you make strategic investments, where dividends or gains are reinvested, those profits generated get ploughed back into the investment to earn more dividends or gains. Over time, your seemingly small savings compounded can amass a substantial sum.

To tap fully into the potential of compound interest, consider the following:

- **Start Early**: Time allows compound interest to flourish. So start investing as early as possible.

- **Reinvest**: Instead of taking the profits out, reinvest them. This powers the compounding machine.

- **Keep Investing**: Regularly add to your investment so that the principal keeps growing.

- **Be Patient**: The compounding results are not immediate, they grow over time.

Albert Einstein identified the potential of compound interest, a small tool with significant implications. Put your funds in the right areas, and let the eighth wonder of the world—compound interest, work its magic on your financial health. Time, patience, and knowledge of compounding can unlock significant wealth that may be instrumental in realising your financial goals. Grasp the power of compound interest, seek its rewards, and ensure your path to financial success is firmly rooted.

Chapter 9. Investment Strategies: Active vs. Passive

In any journey to discover and understand the intricacies of investment strategies, one of the foundational concepts upon which you'll inevitably stumble is that of active and passive investment. It is this dualism that forms the bedrock of many investment portfolios, and understanding the underlying philosophies and techniques of both is crucial as you stride towards your financial goals.

9.1. Active Investing

In the realm of investing, active investing is akin to the hare in the classic fable. It is dynamic, constantly on the move, driven by the relentless pursuit of astounding results. That pursuit is accomplished smoothly or, at times, roughshod over various market trends and conditions.

Active investing is built upon the belief that financial markets are inefficient and due to these inefficiencies, there are opportunities to profit. The very crux of active investing is buying and selling investments frequently with the intention of outperforming a specific index or benchmark. This means that the investments are handpicked, with each investment carefully evaluated by the fund manager.

Active investing often involves rigorous research and analysis in quest of the Holy Grail of investing — alpha. Alpha represents the excess returns of a fund relative to the return of a benchmark index. The whole aim of active management is chasing this elusive entity, to provide returns that can beat the market.

Active investors are typically supported by a team of analysts who spend their time scrutinizing economic reports, financial statements, industry trends, and even geopolitics, hunting down every hint of an advantageous investment opportunity.

9.2. Advantages of Active Investing

Active investing shines during a market downturn, and it's at these times that active managers can truly prove their worth. This is because the fate of an actively managed fund is not directly tethered to the state of the broader market, protecting it - and by extension, your investments - when the markets nosedive.

You might also perceive active investing as a way to achieve goals beyond financial growth. For example, some investors might use an active investment strategy to pursue social or environmental objectives by proactively excluding companies that don't meet specific ethical or sustainability criteria.

Despite higher costs, active management, when carried out well, can often prove its value during volatile markets or within less efficient market sectors where opportunities to outperform are more frequent.

9.3. Disadvantages of Active Investing

The pursuit of higher returns with active investing comes at a cost – literally. Ongoing fees are higher due to the administrative costs, trading costs and other transaction fees, which could erode returns. Plus, successful forecasting is no easy task. It requires skill, experience, and a bit of luck. To consistently outperform the market is a tremendous challenge even for the most seasoned fund managers.

Additionally, active management embodies another risk: the human factor. Emotions and biases can sometimes guide investment decisions, potentially leading to irrational behaviors and suboptimal outcomes.

9.4. Passive Investing

If active investing is the hare, then meet the tortoise: passive investing. It is the embodiment of a more laid-back, patient approach to wealth creation. Instead of trying to beat the market, passive investors aim to match the market performance.

Passively managed funds track a market index, sector, commodity, or other collection of assets. The goal here is not to find the winners but rather to hold a broad basket of investments populated by hundreds—sometimes even thousands—of securities. Such a strategy is built on the axiom that over time, overall market performance will provide a good rate of return and compound into substantial wealth.

9.5. Advantages of Passive Investing

One of the main advantages of passive investing is its lower cost when compared to active investing. Since the approach is more "hands-off," requiring fewer fund manager decisions and transaction activity, the associated costs are substantially reduced.

Passive investing embraces diversification, protecting your nest egg from the particular risks associated with individual stocks. It spreads the investment over a wide range of assets, lowering the potential of facing significant losses due to single poor-performing stocks.

Another point in passive investing's favor is consistency. This approach keeps emotions at bay as ties to specific companies or industry biases have less room to roam, potentially mitigating less optimal outcomes driven by sentiment.

9.6. Disadvantages of Passive Investing

While passive investing is sturdy and reliable, it does have its share of obstacles. For one, it is poised to mirror the market's return but will never have an opportunity to outperform it.

When the market goes down, passively managed funds will go with it as well, resulting in decline. In such instances, the losses can be significantly higher than what you might witness in an actively managed fund.

Since passive investing includes all types of businesses within an index—with no regard to their financial health or market outlook—it may mean that you end up supporting companies or sectors that don't align with your values.

9.7. Summary

Both active and passive strategies have their place in an investment portfolio. What matters is understanding how each works and determining what aligns most effectively with your finances, goals, risk tolerance, and personal beliefs. As you start your investment journey, remember that there isn't a one-size-fits-all strategy. Be patient, learn continuously, and evolve your approach as you gain more knowledge, experience, and confidence.

Next time in the financial jungle, remember: be it the patient tortoise or the speedy hare, the race to financial prosperity is not always won by the fleetest but by those who know where they're going. With the right knowledge and strategies, you can indeed find your personal path to financial success.

Chapter 10. Retirement Ready: Wise Investment for Your Golden Years

Investing for retirement can feel daunting, but it doesn't have to be. The key is to start as early as possible, but it's never too late to begin. Here's a step-by-step guide on how to invest wisely for your golden years.

10.1. Understanding Your Retirement Goals

Recognizing what you want your retirement to look like is the first step toward wise investment. Before investing any money, spend some time reflecting on your retirement goals. Write down everything from retirement age and lifestyle to your plan for unexpected expenses and budgeting for more routine costs. This will foster a clear idea of what you'll need to save in order to achieve your goals.

10.2. Know Your Time Horizon

Time horizon refers to the amount of time that your money will be invested before you need to start withdrawing it. Knowing your time horizon can help guide your investment decisions. If you're young and decades away from retirement, you can afford to take more investment risks. As you get closer to retirement, you may want to move more of your portfolio into less risky investments.

10.3. Diversification of Your Retirement Portfolio

Diversification is a key strategy for retirement investments. It involves spreading your money across different types of investments to help minimize risk. In terms of retirement investing, this might mean distributing your investments among stocks, bonds, mutual funds, real estate, and possibly more alternative assets like precious metals or cryptocurrencies.

10.4. The Role of Fixed-Income Assets

Fixed-income assets, such as bonds and CDs, provide steady and predictable income, which can be a necessary component of a retirement portfolio. They balance out riskier holdings like stocks. As you near retirement, it's generally recommended to shift more of your portfolio into fixed-income assets.

10.5. The Importance of Equity Investments

Equities, or stocks, have historically provided higher returns than other asset classes over the long term. When you're younger and your retirement date is far off, equities should typically make up a larger portion of your portfolio. However, remember that with these higher returns comes increased risk, and as you approach retirement, you'll want to slowly reduce the proportion of equities in your portfolio.

10.6. Maintaining Proper Asset Allocation

Your asset allocation—the way you divide your investments among different asset types—can significantly impact your portfolio's risk level and potential return. Ideally, you should review and adjust your asset allocation at least once a year, or whenever there are significant changes in your life or financial goals.

10.7. Managing Risk vs. Return

In investing, risk and potential return have a direct relationship—the higher the potential return, the greater the risk. Try to find a balance where you are comfortable with the level of risk but still able to achieve the returns you need to meet your goals. This balance is different for everyone and will likely change as you age and get closer to retirement.

10.8. Inflation and its impact on Retirement Savings

Inflation can significantly erode the purchasing power of your money over time. Therefore, you need to consider it when planning for retirement. Invest in assets that can potentially outpace inflation, such as equity investments or real estate, or consider inflation-protected assets like Treasury Inflation-Protected Securities (TIPS).

10.9. Emergency Savings and Healthcare

As you plan for retirement, don't forget to consider unexpected expenses, including healthcare costs. You don't want a medical emergency to drain your retirement savings. It's a good idea to have an emergency fund and consider investing in a Health Savings Account (HSA) or long-term care insurance.

10.10. Importance of Rebalancing

Over time, some investments will perform better than others which can skew your asset allocation. Rebalancing helps you stay in line with your desired risk level and investment strategy. While it's important not to overdo it, a review once or twice per year is often enough.

10.11. Tax-Advantaged Retirement Accounts

Don't overlook the role of tax-advantaged retirement accounts like 401(k)s and IRAs. These vehicles offer unique tax benefits that can help you grow your money faster.

10.12. The Role of Professional Financial Advice

While there's a lot you can do on your own, a financial advisor can provide valuable guidance, especially as you navigate the complexities of retirement planning. Choose an advisor who understands your goals and is aligned with your interests.

Remember, starting early, thinking long-term, assessing your risk tolerance, diversifying your investments, and regularly reviewing and rebalancing your portfolio can go a long way in creating a flourishing retirement fund. Investing wisely for your sunset years may seem challenging, but with careful planning and disciplined execution, you can navigate your way to a comfortable and secure retirement.

Chapter 11. Maintaining Your Portfolio in Changing Times

The world of investing is not a static one. By nature, it is continuously evolving, reflecting broader economic conditions, development of new industries, and technology innovations. The key to maintaining a robust portfolio amidst these fluctuations is to regularly evaluate it in line with your financial objectives.

11.1. Importance of Portfolio Maintenance

Constant change is the new normal in our world. Economic conditions, political landscapes, and global events can impact the investment world in ways both big and small. Therefore, keeping your finger on the pulse of your investments and making adjustments when necessary is crucial. This concept is at the heart of portfolio maintenance.

Portfolio maintenance allows you to keep track of your investments, identifying what's working for you and what isn't. It provides an opportunity to reallocate funds based on changing circumstances and ensures your portfolio aligns with your risk tolerance and investment objectives.

11.2. Reviewing Your Investment Portfolio

Reviewing your portfolio involves evaluating investment performance, analyzing market trends and economic conditions, and assessing whether the combination of assets within your portfolio continues to meet your financial goals.

A review should be conducted at least annually. However, more frequent reviews may be necessary depending on the nature of your investments and current market conditions. Consider employing a schedule that aligns with your comfort level and ensures attention to all your investment holdings.

While reviewing your portfolio, scrutinize the return on each investment and compare it with appropriate benchmarks. If an investment continually underperforms without any apparent reason, it may be time to consider a replacement. At the same time, investments that have performed exceptionally well may need to be rebalanced to ensure the proportion of your portfolio is not heavily skewed in one direction.

11.3. Rebalancing Your Investment Portfolio

Rebalancing involves adjusting your portfolio periodically to ensure it aligns with your desired asset allocation. The primary purpose of rebalancing is to mitigate risk rather than maximize returns.

Over time, depending on their performance, some investments may occupy more or less space in your portfolio than initially intended. For example, if stocks have outperformed bonds in your portfolio, your asset allocation may become stock-heavy. This scenario may expose you to more risk than you initially signed up for. Therefore, to rebalance, you might need to sell some stocks and buy more bonds to restore the initial balance.

Rebalancing can be done in two principal ways: by calendar, for example, semi-annually or annually, or by threshold, when an asset's weight within the portfolio deviates by a predetermined percentage from the original asset allocation.

Remember, when rebalancing, it is essential to factor in taxes, trading costs, and any penalties associated early withdrawal. It might be advantageous to rebalance using new money coming into the portfolio, whether regular contributions or dividends, to avoid these costs and maintain the desired allocation.

11.4. Incorporating Diversification

Maintaining a diverse portfolio is a proven strategy to mitigate risk. By spreading your investments across a variety of asset classes, such as equities, fixed income (bonds), cash, commodities, and alternative investments, you can cushion your portfolio against market volatility.

However, keep in mind that diversification isn't a one-time task when initially building your portfolio. It's a ongoing process. As markets change, the diversity of your portfolio may also need to shift. Regular reviews will help identify where adjustments are needed.

While investing entirely in equities might fetch higher returns during a bullish market, the risk is also significantly higher. Therefore, incorporating bonds, cash investments, or other securities can provide a safety net during a market downturn.

11.5. Managing Emotional Investing

It's natural for investors to become influenced by market news, leading to panic or over-enthusiasm. This emotional investing can often lead to poor decision-making.

When markets are booming, and everyone seems to be making money, it can be tempting to jump on the bandwagon and invest more than you should. Conversely, during a market downturn, it might feel right to sell investments to 'stop the bleeding.' However, these decisions, often made based on emotions, can be counterproductive in the long run.

Maintaining a clear investment strategy, based on logic and careful analysis, can help reduce emotional reactions. Regular portfolio reviews can guide these decisions.

Portfolio maintenance, therefore, is a multifaceted process that must be rooted in the realities of changing times. Regular, informed adjustments are vital in ensuring your portfolio stays on track and continues to work towards achieving your financial goals. Bearing the concepts of portfolio review, rebalancing, diversification, and emotional management in mind can provide you the tools to navigate the often turbulent waters of investing, ensuring not just survival, but prosperity.